WHAT'S THE DEAL?

Prescription Drug Abuse

Karla Fitzhugh

www.heinemann.co.uk/library

Visit our website to find out more information about Heinemann Library books.

To order:
Phone 44 (0) 1865 888066
Send a fax to 44 (0) 1865 314091
Visit the Heinemann Bookshop at www.heinemann.co.uk/library to browse our catalogue and order online.

Produced for Heinemann Library by White-Thomson Publishing Ltd, Bridgewater Business Centre, 210 High Street, Lewes, East Sussex, BN7 2NH.

First published in Great Britain by Heinemann Library, Jordan Hill, Oxford OX2 8EJ, part of Harcourt Education.

Heinemann Library is a registered trademark of Harcourt Education Ltd.

Consultant: Jenny McWhirter, Head of Education and Prevention, DrugScope
Editorial: Clare Collinson
Design: Tim Mayer
Picture Research: Elaine Fuoco-Lang
Production: Duncan Gilbert

Originated by P.T. Repro Multi Warna
Printed and bound in China, by South China Printing Company.

The paper used to print this book comes from sustainable resources.

The case studies and quotations in this book are based on factual examples. However, in some cases, the names or other personal information have been changed to protect the privacy of the individual concerned.

10 digit ISBN 0 431 10783 1 (hardback)
13 digit ISBN 978 0 431 10783 7 (hardback)
10 09 08 07 06
10 9 8 7 6 5 4 3 2 1

10 digit ISBN 0 431 10795 5 (paperback)
13 digit ISBN 978 0 431 10795 0 (paperback)
11 10 09 08 07
10 9 8 7 6 5 4 3 2 1

British Library Cataloguing in Publication Data
Fitzhugh, Karla
Prescription drug abuse. – (What's the deal?)
1. Drugs – Juvenile literature 2. Medication abuse – Juvenile literature
I. Title
362.2'99
A full catalogue record for this book is available from the British Library.

Acknowledgements
The publisher would like to thank the following for their kind permission to use their photographs:

Alamy Images **15**, **32–33**; Corbis (Ric Ergenbright) **19**, (Hekimian Julian/Corbis Sygma) **36**, (Ted Horowitz) **10**, (Richard Hutchings) **39**, (Left Lane Productions) **11**, (LWA–Stephen Welstead) **44**, (Richard T. Nowitz) **32**, (Jose Luis Pelaez, Inc) **4–5**, (Mark Peterson) **46**, (David Pollack) **30**, (Bob Rowan; Progressive Image) **37**, (Chuck Savage) **8**, **23**, (Uwe Schmid) **40–41**, (Ariel Skelley) **13**, (Tom Stewart) **20**; Rex (Airio) **43**, (Burger/Phanie) **18**, (Chat) **29**, (Garo/Phanie) **42**, **49**, (Peter Hosking) **21**, (Greg Mathieson) **16–17**, (Phanie Agency) **24**, (Reso) **34–35**, (Ray Roberts) **31**; Topfoto (The Image Works/Topham) **6**, **7**, **9**, **12**, **14**, **25**, **27**, **28**, **50**.

Cover artwork by Phil Weyman, Kralinator Design.

Every effort has been made to contact copyright holders of any material reproduced in this book. Any omissions will be rectified in subsequent printings if notice is given to the publishers.

Contents

Prescription drug abuse – what's the deal? 4

Prescription drugs today 6

What is prescription drug abuse? 8

Why do people abuse prescription drugs? 10

What is addiction? 12

Prescription drugs and the law 14

Opiates 18

Stimulants 24

Sedatives 30

Anabolic steroids 36

Ketamine 40

Are other prescription drugs abused? 42

Wider effects 44

Can drug abuse and addiction be prevented? 46

Giving up prescription drugs 48

Help and advice 50

Glossary 52

Contacts and further information 54

Index 56

❚ Words appearing in the text in bold, **like this**, are explained in the Glossary.

Prescription drug abuse – what's the deal?

Over the last one hundred years or so, **prescription** drugs have made a great difference to people's health all around the world. Most people who take prescription drugs use them responsibly, as directed by a doctor or dentist. But sometimes people are tempted to take medical drugs for non-medical reasons. This can be risky for their health and wellbeing. So why do people **abuse** prescription drugs?

Mike needed surgery on his nose after it was broken during an assault. After surgery his doctor gave him a prescription for **opiate** painkillers. He liked the way they made him feel and wanted to keep taking them even after his nose had healed. Later he bought two tablets from a **dealer** at a friend's party.

At first he only bought the drugs occasionally. Then pretty soon this became every week, and then every day. Eventually, he had to admit he was **addicted**. It was a long and difficult struggle to give the drugs up.

"When you're **hooked** you don't care about anything or anyone but getting that next **fix**. Addiction feels to me like a little voice on your shoulder telling you to use the drugs and trying to make you think it's OK. Now the voice is much smaller, but it will always be there. Being **clean** is great ... I am grateful that I got out when I did. I take the future one day at a time and know that as long as I don't use drugs things can only get better."

Once you start abusing prescription drugs your life can quickly become out of control. Like Mike, you might one day be offered prescription drugs by someone you know or by a dealer. What decision would you make?

Making decisions

This book will give you the information you need to make your own decisions about prescription drugs. It looks at why some people abuse prescription drugs and explains how abuse can damage their health and their lives. There are also many issues to think about. What is the best way to tackle the problem of drug abuse and what can be done to help addicts? Let's look at prescription drug abuse and the real harm it can do.

■ What are prescription drugs?

Prescription drugs are medicines that are used to treat illnesses or injuries. They are drugs that can only be obtained when a patient has been given a prescription form signed by a doctor or dentist.

❚ Patients need a signed prescription form from their doctor or dentist to pick up prescription drugs from a pharmacy.

Doctors use many different kinds of **prescription** drugs to treat people with health problems. Whenever a doctor prescribes a drug for a patient he or she gives clear instructions about how the drug should be taken. Taking prescription drugs without this advice is very risky.

Medical use

Prescription drugs are powerful and should only be taken under the direct supervision of a doctor. When a doctor prescribes a drug, he or she is careful to:

- work out the correct dose

- check that the drug won't react with other medicines the patient may be taking

- tell the patient exactly how and when to take the drug

- warn the patient about possible unwanted **side effects** and the risks of mixing the drug with alcohol

- watch out for signs of **addiction**.

Many people use prescription drugs every day for common health problems. Inhalers are used to treat asthma.

What is non-medical drug use?

Some people are tempted to use medical drugs when they are not being treated for an illness. This is sometimes called drug **abuse**, **recreational use**, or drug **misuse**. Taking a drug without the advice of a doctor is dangerous. It is easy to take too much (an **overdose**) and suffer unpleasant side effects. Taking different drugs at the same time can cause a deadly reaction, and so can mixing some drugs with alcohol. Once people have started taking these drugs, they may find they are unable to stop. This is called addiction or **dependence**.

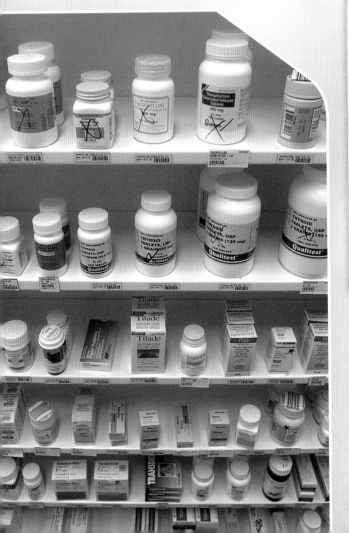

⚠ Commonly abused prescription drugs

These are the most common types of prescription drug that are abused:

- **opiates**: a group of drugs that are used to stop people feeling pain, especially after accidents or surgery

- **stimulants**: a group of drugs that speed up brain activity and make people feel more awake

- **sedatives**: a group of drugs that slow brain activity down and make people feel sleepy or less anxious

- **anabolic steroids**: a group of drugs that affect growth, and can also cause changes like those that happen to boys at **puberty**. Some people abuse steroids because they think they will improve their looks or sports performance.

❚ A huge range of prescription drugs have been developed to treat all kinds of illnesses, enabling people to live active, healthy lives.

7

What is prescription drug abuse?

Most people who are prescribed drugs by a doctor take them responsibly and do not **abuse** them. Unfortunately, some people do abuse **prescription** drugs. Sometimes people become **addicted** to drugs that have been prescribed for them. Other people may obtain prescription drugs illegally.

Patterns of abuse

Patients who are prescribed drugs by their doctor sometimes take them more often and in larger doses than the doctor has told them to. Sometimes they continue to take the drugs when they no longer need them, after their illness has been treated. A few people who take their prescription drugs as directed by a doctor become addicted to or **dependent** on the drugs. You can read more about addiction and dependence on pages 12–13.

Some people abuse prescription drugs that they have obtained illegally. Young people may try them once, just to see what it feels like. Others may take the drugs once every few weeks for a while, and then decide they don't want to use them any more. Other people abuse prescription drugs more regularly and may take large amounts of them. Once they start this pattern of abuse it can be hard for them to stop.

A few people take many different drugs, including prescription medicines and street drugs such as heroin. They may also mix these drugs with alcohol, which can be very dangerous. Sometimes people

❚ Female patients are more likely to be given prescription drugs, and are more at risk of becoming addicted to certain types.

use prescription drugs as a substitute for other drugs. For example, when people who are addicted to heroin cannot obtain any heroin, they may abuse **opiate** painkillers or **sedatives** instead.

Where do the drugs come from?

Sometimes patients may lie to their doctors to persuade them that they need more drugs. They may also hand over fake prescriptions to **pharmacists** or they may visit several doctors to obtain multiple prescriptions. Some people may steal prescription drugs from relatives, pharmacies, hospitals, or factories. People also buy prescription drugs from **dealers** on the street or at parties. Some street drugs are not genuine prescription drugs. They may have been made in illegal laboratories or factories.

▌Most young people do not abuse prescription drugs, but teenage girls are more likely to try them than boys.

■ Who abuses prescription drugs?

There is no "typical" person who abuses prescription drugs. They could be young or old, rich or poor.

- In most Western countries, the people most likely to abuse prescription drugs are aged between 18 and 25.

- Among those aged between twelve and seventeen, girls are more likely to abuse prescription drugs than boys. These girls mainly abuse **stimulants** and sedatives.

9

Why do people abuse prescription drugs?

The causes of **prescription** drug **abuse** are very complicated. It may be tempting to think of drugs as a solution to a problem, but in reality they are often likely to cause new problems.

Different influences

There are many things that can influence people to start abusing prescription drugs. Some people simply try a drug out of curiosity. They may have heard or read about it and wonder what it is like. Often, they do not know much about the drug and do not understand the risks. Other people try drugs because they like to take risks. Some people see drugs as an escape from bad feelings or situations. However, abusing drugs does not make the problems go away, and often causes new ones.

Fitting in with the group?

If a young person's friends are abusing prescription drugs, they may start taking them too. This could be because they want to fit in with the group. It may also be because their friends have given them bad advice about how safe the drugs are. This is sometimes called **peer influence** or **peer pressure**.

❚ Friends sometimes dress or act in a certain way to fit in with a group.

I Teenagers often worry about being left out of group activities, or losing their friends.

The effects of the drugs

Many people abuse prescription drugs because they want to get a certain effect. Some people feel stressed, anxious, or depressed, and take prescription drugs without medical advice because they think the drugs will make them feel better. This is called "self-medicating". Only a qualified doctor or dentist has the skills to decide whether someone needs prescription medication or not.

Some people abuse prescription drugs such as **anabolic steroids** and **stimulants** because they think these drugs will help to change the way they look. However, changes such as this are short-lived. The drugs can cause unpleasant **side effects**, such as skin problems and baldness. Some people abuse prescription drugs to reduce the unpleasant effects of other drugs. For example, stimulants keep people awake for hours, so some users take **sedatives** as well to help them sleep. Mixing drugs in this way is especially dangerous. Other people take prescription drugs because they have become **dependent** on them and feel they cannot stop taking them.

Cheating at sports

Sometimes people abuse anabolic steroids because they think they will improve their sports performance. Using drugs to try to win at sport is cheating. You can read more about the effects and risks of taking anabolic steroids on pages 36–39.

Some people who take **prescription** drugs find it very difficult to give them up. Their bodies or minds become used to the drugs, and they need to take more to get the same effect. The drugs may start to control their whole lives.

What does "addiction" mean?

Addiction or **dependence** is when a person has an unhealthy habit that they feel unable to give up. This habit could be anything from smoking cigarettes to **abusing** prescription drugs, gambling, or drinking too much alcohol. Some drugs, such as **sedatives** and certain painkillers, can cause physical addiction. This is when the person's body becomes so used to the drug that when the person stops using it, they become physically ill with **withdrawal symptoms**. For example, they may have flu-like symptoms or stomach upsets, or they may start shaking.

People may also develop mental or **psychological dependence** on drugs. This is when people use drugs to get through everyday life, and feel that they cannot cope with life without them. Psychological dependence is more common than physical addiction and can happen with any drug.

▌**Pharmacists** are careful to check that prescriptions are not false or stolen. They also look out for patients who might be addicted to their medication.

A person's drug use can cause conflict with anyone who is close to them.

Signs of addiction

Early signs of addiction may include a person:

- spending long periods every day thinking about the drug

- feeling they need the drug just to get through the day

- becoming anxious if they can't get hold of the drug

- being secretive about what they are doing

- becoming angry when someone challenges them about their drug use

- missing lots of school or work

- stealing from family or friends to get the money they need to buy drugs.

Viewpoints

Some people criticize doctors for handing out too many prescriptions for addictive drugs. Others disagree and say doctors are now very aware of how to prevent addiction.

- **Doctors do everything they can to help prevent addiction**
Nowadays, doctors monitor their patients very closely and prescribe only the necessary dose. They prescribe alternative non-addictive drugs if possible. Many people who become addicted to prescription drugs obtain the drugs illegally and a doctor is not involved.

- **Doctors do not do enough to prevent addiction**
Some doctors still do not know enough about the problems of addiction and abuse. They prescribe too many addictive drugs and do not always explain the risks to their patients. When patients are addicted, doctors do not do enough to help them give up the drugs.

What do you think?

Certain drugs have been classed as **prescription** drugs by law because they can cause serious health problems or **addiction**. It is illegal for someone to use them without the permission of a doctor, or to give or sell them to someone else. Not knowing about the law is no excuse as far as the courts are concerned. Having a criminal record related to drug use can seriously affect a person's future.

Prescription drug crimes

The crimes associated with prescription drug **abuse** include:

- unlawful **possession**: this means that someone has in their possession a prescription drug that hasn't been prescribed for them by a doctor

- **supply**: this means selling or giving a drug to another person or other people –

Carrying drugs that were not prescribed for you is illegal, and can lead to arrest.

Opiates (also called opoids) are a group of drugs that are commonly prescribed to relieve pain. This group of medicines includes the drugs morphine and codeine as well as many other related drugs. They are sometimes called **narcotics**.

What do doctors use them for?

Strong opiates such as morphine are often given to patients before or after surgery. They are also used to relieve cancer-related pain or pain from broken bones. Weaker opiates such as codeine may be given for headaches or mild pains in the joints. These drugs tend to be given in tablet form or by injection. Opiates can cause constipation and sleepiness. In large doses they can slow down a person's breathing. When someone takes opiates, it is essential that they follow the instructions of a doctor. Doctors give just enough of the drug to reduce a person's level of pain. They know that giving more than this amount can lead to **addiction** or **overdose**.

How do opiates work?

Once inside the body, the drug molecules attach to special areas called "opiate receptor sites" in the cells of the brain and spine. This stops pain messages from being sent to the parts of the brain that normally sense pain. The street drug heroin also acts in this way. **Prescription** painkiller **abuse** can be just as dangerous as heroin abuse.

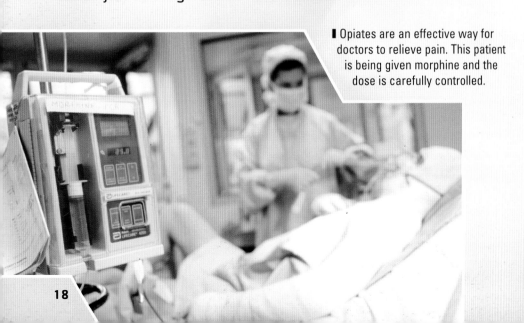

❚ Opiates are an effective way for doctors to relieve pain. This patient is being given morphine and the dose is carefully controlled.

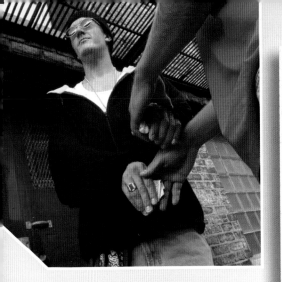

Selling drugs illegally can lead to heavy fines and time in prison.

selling a drug to others for money or swapping drugs for other goods is also known as **dealing**

- **trafficking**: this means transporting drugs, usually in large amounts, and selling them to others

- **illegal manufacture**: this means making certain drugs without a government licence. Sometimes illegally manufactured drugs are fakes. Selling fake drugs is still an offence.

Penalties

If someone is caught unlawfully possessing prescription drugs they may be given a formal warning or caution by the police. They may also be charged, fined, and sent to prison, especially if they have committed a drug offence before. Supplying drugs is considered a more serious offence and can lead to harsher penalties. Penalties vary depending on the type of drug involved. You can read more about prescription drug laws and penalties on pages 16–17.

Viewpoints

These are disagreements about the best way to deal with people who abuse prescription drugs. There are strong opinions on both sides.

- **Drug abusers should be given medical treatment rather than prison sentences**
  In prison, drug offenders are unlikely to get treatment for their addiction and they may still be able to obtain drugs. Sending them to prison will not stop them taking drugs.

- **Prescription drug abuse is a crime and, like other crimes, it should be punished**
  Drug abusers are criminals and other people should be protected from them. People will also be less likely to abuse prescription drugs if they know they will be sent to jail if they are caught.

What do you think?

Opiate abuse

When prescription opiates are abused, they may come from a doctor, or they may be stolen. They may also be bought from drug **dealers** who sometimes sell non-medical opiates such as heroin too. People who can't get one kind of opiate often try a different kind, and may start taking stronger and stronger ones. People who abuse prescription opiates tend to call the drugs by their brand names, such as OxyContin, or shortened versions of them, like "oxy". Sometimes they are given names like "kicker" and "hillbilly heroin". Tablets are chewed, crushed and **snorted** (sniffed), or dissolved and injected. All these practices can kill. People may think that drugs from the doctor are somehow "safe", but this is not true.

! Opiate abuse is increasing

Prescription painkiller abuse is on the rise in the United States. Many users are not aware of how powerful and dangerous these drugs can be. In the last fifteen years, the number of new opiate users has tripled. The number of deaths caused by overdoses of prescription drugs has also increased.

❚ Drugs such as morphine and heroin are made from the pods of opium poppies.

Dangerous side effects

People who take **opiates** may experience dangerous **side effects**. Opiates tend to cause a drowsy, sleepy feeling. This is dangerous for a number of reasons. It can make it impossible for someone to drive a car safely or to operate machinery. Riding a bicycle in traffic can also be risky. Spending a large part of the day in a sleepy state also makes it difficult to have a normal life. Relationships can be ruined, and work and education may suffer. Large doses of opiates can also cause nausea (feeling queasy or sick) and vomiting. If someone is very drowsy from taking opiates and they vomit, they might choke in their sleep. This can cause serious harm and may even be fatal.

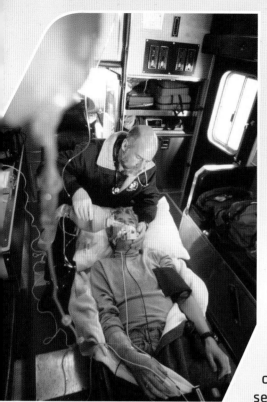

❚ Opiate abuse can cause fatal overdoses.

Overdoses

If people take opiates without following the instructions of a doctor, there is a much greater chance of them taking an **overdose**. When this happens, breathing starts to slow down to dangerously low levels, and the brain and body are starved of oxygen. This can cause permanent brain damage and sometimes death. The signs of an opiate overdose include:

■ pinprick-sized pupils in the eyes

■ clammy skin

■ convulsions (fits)

■ **coma** (deep unconsciousness).

There is no way to know how strong an opiate will be if it is obtained illegally. This means it is very easy to take an overdose.

Question

What happens if a pregnant woman abuses opiates?

Some illegally sold drugs are fakes. Others are mixed with a wide variety of cheaper chemicals so the sellers can make a bigger profit. Sometimes these chemicals can be very harmful.

▌Prescription drugs can be even more dangerous if they are injected.

Emergency action

If you think someone has taken an overdose of opiates, call for an ambulance immediately. The person will need medical treatment right away, or he or she could die. Doctors may be able to give the person a drug that can reverse the effects of the opiates.

The dangers of injecting opiates

Injecting drugs damages veins and causes infections and scar tissue. If people share needles, infections in one person's blood can easily be passed on to another person. This means that infections such as **HIV** (the virus that causes AIDS) and **hepatitis B** or **C** (which cause liver disease) can spread between users.

Answer

There is an increased chance of stillbirth (when the baby is born dead), or the baby could be very small when it is born. The baby may also be born **addicted** to opiates.

Are opiates addictive?

When someone who does not need pain relief takes **opiates** without the advice of a doctor, there is a strong chance that they will become **addicted**. The longer someone **abuses prescription** opiates, the greater the chance that they will become both physically addicted and **psychologically dependent**. Imagine what it would be like if drugs controlled your whole life.

Becoming hooked

Addiction to opiates can creep up on people, as they develop a **tolerance** to the drug. This happens as their bodies get used to the drugs and they need larger and larger doses to get the same effect. They may not realize that they have a problem until it is too late. People who are physically addicted to opiates need the drugs just to "feel normal" and they experience unpleasant **withdrawal symptoms** if they stop taking the drugs.

People who are addicted to opiates experience **cravings**, or strong urges to take more of the drug. They may start to do desperate things to get the money they need for a regular supply of drugs. They may lie and steal money from their families and friends or commit burglaries. They may neglect many things, including their families, their friends, their general health, and personal hygiene.

*"The first day with no drugs I thought, 'This isn't so bad, I can handle this.' Then the second day my nose started running uncontrollably. It was one hundred degrees outside and I had goose bumps, shivering like it's cold, even though I was pouring sweat. The third day I got the worst case of diarrhoea I have ever had. The fourth day my joints started to hurt. Also throughout the whole thing I had mood swings of severe anxiety or depression. I've been **clean** for a month now and plan on staying that way."*

Tyler, aged twenty

What are withdrawal symptoms?

If someone who is addicted to opiates cannot get the drugs, they become anxious, restless, and irritable. If someone stops taking the drugs completely, they go on to suffer full withdrawal symptoms. These include:

- flu-like symptoms: watery eyes, a runny nose, and loss of appetite

- pains and cramps in the muscles

- difficulty sleeping or resting

- feelings of panic

- shakes, chills, and sweating

- nausea, vomiting, and stomach pains.

The worst of these symptoms are usually over in about a week. If people who are addicted decide to give up drugs, they can be given all kinds of help and support (see pages 48–49).

▌Opiate addicts may turn to crime to fund their habit. They may steal goods and sell them to get money, or swap the goods for drugs.

Stimulants

Stimulants are drugs that speed up reactions in the brain. The most commonly **abused prescription** stimulants are **amphetamines**. Nowadays, amphetamines are not given to many patients, because they are **addictive** and can have bad **side effects**. Most of the amphetamines that are abused are street drugs, made and sold illegally. Illegally sold amphetamines are often referred to as "uppers" or "speed".

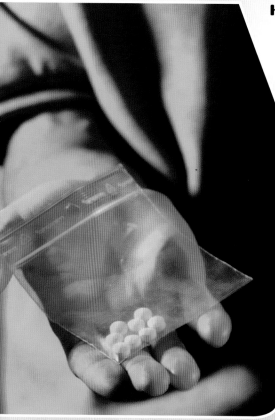

I Most stimulants that are abused are made illegally.

How do stimulants work?

Stimulants work by stimulating the activity of the body's **nervous system**. They increase the amounts of certain chemicals in the brain and make the heart beat faster. This makes people feel wide awake, alert, and able to concentrate more.

What are they prescribed for?

Many years ago, prescription amphetamines were used to treat all kinds of health problems. Then doctors realized that patients were having bad side effects. In some cases, patients took **overdoses** by accident, and others became addicted to their medication. Doctors decided to stop prescribing amphetamines for most of their patients.

Nowadays, stimulant drugs are mainly prescribed for two health problems: narcolepsy and ADHD. Narcolepsy is a condition that causes people to fall asleep suddenly during the day. They have no control over this. Small doses of stimulant drugs help sufferers stay awake during the day. ADHD, or attention deficit hyperactivity disorder, is the name given to a condition that includes a range of behaviour problems. People with ADHD may find it difficult to pay attention to things or concentrate. To help with this problem, children with this condition may be prescribed an amphetamine-like drug called Ritalin. Although Ritalin makes the brain more active, it seems to have a calming effect on children with ADHD.

❚ Drugs such as Ritalin are used to treat children with ADHD who find it difficult to concentrate and are often much more active than other children.

Amphetamine abuse

Most of the amphetamines sold on the street have been made illegally. But some have been stolen from pharmacies, hospitals, or factories, or obtained using a false prescription. The drugs come in pill form, and may be swallowed, or crushed up and **snorted**. Some users prepare them for injection. All these methods of use are dangerous. Crystal meth is one type of street amphetamine. It is a powerful drug that is usually smoked.

Amphetamine abuse is a massive public health problem in Far Eastern countries such as Thailand. Amphetamine abuse is increasing in the United States, Australia, and parts of New Zealand.

> ❗ **Street names for amphetamines**
>
> Street names for amphetamines include: uppers, speed, phets, meth, whizz, pep pills, P, goey, and crank.

What does amphetamine abuse do to the body?

Amphetamine abuse can disrupt normal sleep patterns, leaving people unable to get a good night's rest. Users feel exhausted the next day. It can also lead to people not eating enough food, so they miss out on healthy vitamins and minerals. They may also get stomach pains, diarrhoea, or constipation. Lack of sleep and food can make people seriously run down. Users frequently suffer from bad colds and flu. Some experts believe amphetamine abuse can cause brain damage.

Amphetamine abuse and mental health

Amphetamine abuse can make someone irritable, restless, and stressed out. The more a person takes, the more likely they are to have strong feelings of anxiety and fear. They may also have:

- **panic attacks**, where they feel as if something terrible is about to happen

- feelings of **paranoia**, when they become suspicious for no good reason, or feel that people are "out to get them"

- mood swings – they may become down and depressed, or aggressive and violent.

Large doses of these drugs can also lead to an illness called "amphetamine psychosis". This is where someone becomes very restless and paranoid and has **hallucinations**. There is a risk that they could harm themselves or others.

"I took amphetamines at a party. I was tired, and a friend said I could share his drugs. He said it would help me to wake up. My heart started pounding so hard I thought it was going to burst out of my chest. It was really scary. After that, I had panic attacks. It took me ages to get over it."

Laurence, aged sixteen

Question

What is ephedra?

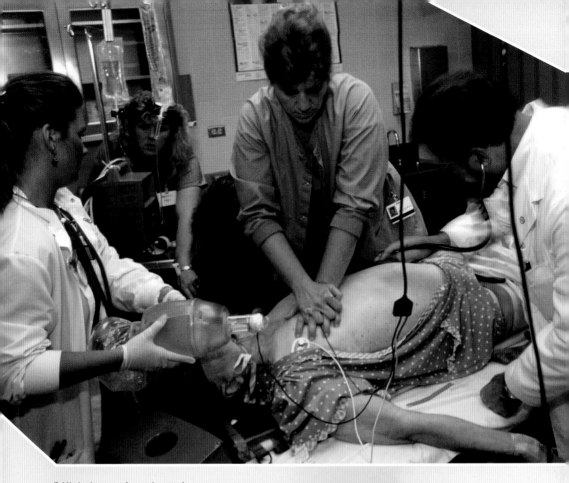

❚ High doses of amphetamines can put a
serious strain on the user's heart and may
even cause death.

Can amphetamines kill you?

Large doses of amphetamines can
speed the heart up so much that it
makes it beat in an irregular way.
When this happens, the heart
cannot pump blood around the body
properly, and the user may die.
Mixing amphetamines with other
drugs, even those that seem
harmless, can also kill. For example,
mixing amphetamines with some
cold remedies may cause a
dangerously irregular heartbeat, or
a fatal rise in blood pressure.

Answer

Ephedra, or Ma Huang,
is a **stimulant** drug
that is banned in many
countries. It may be
found in bodybuilding
or diet products, or in
herbal tonics. It has
been linked to several
deaths and can cause
harm to unborn babies
during pregnancy.

What's in street amphetamines?

Amphetamines prescribed by doctors are made in factories under controlled conditions. Each tablet contains a known amount of the drug and other ingredients. The drugs are made under clean conditions, so nothing else gets into them. Even though they have been made legally, it is still very dangerous to **abuse** these drugs because of their powerful effects. Illegally-made street drugs have the same dangers, plus a whole lot more.

❚ Some users continue to take stimulants because they feel unable to cope without them.

Daniel's story

Nineteen-year-old Daniel was prescribed Ritalin when he was fifteen because he was having difficulty concentrating at school. He soon found he was taking too much.

"When I was fifteen years old, I was put on Ritalin. Today I am still picking up the pieces after my life was shattered by this drug. I became addicted to Ritalin almost immediately. I only took the prescribed dose at first, but soon began taking more to keep me from going into deep depressions."

Nowadays, many doctors prefer not to prescribe Ritalin to teenagers, because of the possible risks of **side effects** and addiction.

▮ Giving up amphetamines can be a real struggle once someone has become dependent on them.

Street amphetamines are made out of **toxic** chemicals in dirty conditions. After they have been made, they are often mixed with other chemicals to bulk them out. This makes more profit for the drug **dealers**. Street amphetamines can be 95 per cent pure or 5 per cent pure. You can't tell how pure they are or what's in them just by looking. There is also the chance that they might contain something poisonous.

Tolerance to amphetamines

When someone takes amphetamines regularly, they may start to build up a **tolerance** to the drugs, so they need to take larger and larger doses to get the same effect. When doctors give **stimulants** to patients, they always monitor them carefully to make sure they are not developing tolerance.

Are amphetamines addictive?

There is some disagreement among experts about whether amphetamines cause physical **addiction**. However, all experts agree amphetamines can lead to strong **psychological dependence**. Users may keep taking the drugs because they feel that they cannot cope with everyday life without them. Or they may keep taking the drugs to avoid the feelings they get when they stop taking them. These feelings include tiredness, stress, depression, and incredibly strong sensations of hunger.

Sedatives are drugs that act on the brain and body to slow them down. They are also called **depressants**. Doctors sometimes prescribe sedatives to patients who are feeling anxious or having difficulty sleeping. They should never be taken without the advice of a doctor because they are **addictive** and they can kill.

Sedatives and their actions

The best-known medicines in this group are **synthetic** drugs called **minor tranquillizers**. These drugs increase the amount of a chemical in the brain that slows down brain activity. When used in the amounts recommended by a doctor, this can have a calming effect or can cause a sleepy feeling. Sedatives may help people who are feeling anxious or who are unable to sleep. They may also be given for muscle spasms. They are supposed to be short-term treatments. Drugs are not normally the best way to solve long-term problems with anxiety and sleeplessness. Most doctors only prescribe these drugs to a patient for a few days.

▌A short course of tranquillizers may help people who have serious difficulty sleeping.

! **Street names for sedatives**

Street names for sedatives include: downers, sleepers, tranx, benzos, or versions of brand names such as Valium.

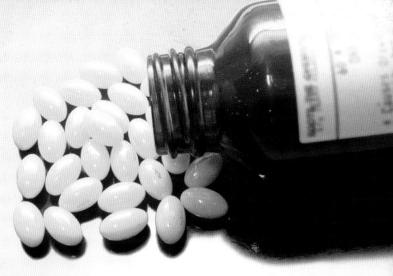

Doctors only prescribe tranquillizers for short periods of time, because they can be addictive.

Minor tranquillizers

Most minor tranquillizers are drugs called **benzodiazepines**. There are many different kinds of drugs in this group. Some of them are stronger than others and some have effects that last longer than others. They can have many unwanted **side effects**, and **abuse** of these drugs is very dangerous. They can cause addiction, **overdose**, and harm to the body and mind.

Tranquillizer abuse

Many people who are addicted to tranquillizers are patients who have been prescribed them for years. Doctors do not prescribe them so often anymore because they now realize how addictive these drugs can be. The benzodiazepines that are sold illegally tend to be medical drugs. People lie to doctors to get them, then abuse the drugs themselves or sell them to others. Sometimes they are stolen from pharmacies, hospitals, or factories.

"Benzodiazepines made me down, depressed, and sleepy. I couldn't be bothered to do much, even cook a meal. You can't remember things, but it's much more than brief forgetfulness. My children are now twelve and fourteen and I don't remember a large part of the time when they were growing up. The memories are completely gone, it's frustrating for yourself and the people around you. It's quite tragic really."

Judith, who was addicted to benzodiazepines for eight years

What are the risks?

Tranquillizers can have many dangers. Because **benzodiazepines** slow down brain activity, they can cause drowsiness. This can make it dangerous to operate machinery or drive a car, increasing the risk of serious accidents. Taken in larger amounts, benzodiazepines can result in an **overdose**. This is especially likely if they are mixed with certain other drugs or alcohol. Tranquillizers can slow someone's breathing or heart rate down so much that a person can die.

Some users inject the drugs, increasing the risk of an accidental overdose, as well as damage to veins and serious infections. Injecting the contents of capsules has had terrible effects on some people. In some cases, the drugs can damage the blood vessels and block off the blood flow to various parts of the body. Because of this, people have had their legs or other parts of their bodies amputated.

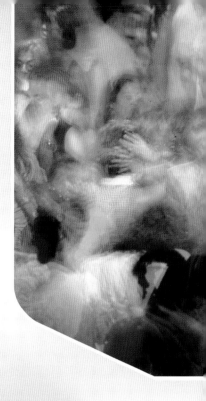

❚ Some people have lost a limb after injecting tranquillizers over a long period of time.

▌ If someone has their drink spiked with sedative drugs, it can make them feel confused, dizzy, and drowsy.

Drug-assisted rape

Recently there have been many cases of sexual assault and rape involving the use of **sedative** drugs on victims. Attackers slip sedatives such as Rohypnol ("roofies") and Gamma Hydroxybutyrate (GHB) into a person's drink or food without them knowing (this is known as "**spiking**"). The drug makes the person very drowsy or even unconscious, so they are helpless and vulnerable to attack. Some people have died after being given these drugs. The victim can be male or female, and there may be one or more attackers. The rapist may be a stranger or somebody the victim already knows. Rape is a very serious crime, and the victims can be severely traumatized. It is thought that one in five rapes involves drugs.

❗ Staying safe

All drinkers need to watch out for people interfering with their drink. There are several things people can do to reduce the risk of drug-assisted rape. They should:

- never accept drinks from strangers

- never take drink from punchbowls at parties

- never share drinks with other people

- always keep drinks in their hand in public places or at parties

- buy bottled drinks and keep the lid on them when not drinking out of them

- never leave drinks unattended

- stop drinking a drink if it looks or tastes strange

- take the drink with them if they need to go to the toilet, or get a fresh one when they return.

Remember, if you see someone putting something in another person's drink, always warn the person. It can be very dangerous.

Side effects of tranquillizers

Sedative drugs have very powerful effects on the activity of the brain. There are many possible **side effects**, especially if someone uses **tranquillizers** for a long time. This is one of the reasons why doctors only prescribe them for short periods. The side effects of sedatives include:

- confusion or memory problems

- mood swings and sudden aggression

- dizziness and shaky walking

- diarrhoea, constipation, nausea, vomiting, and stomach pains

- headaches and visual problems.

Tranquillizers and addiction

Using these drugs for longer periods leads to **tolerance** developing, where the person needs more and more drugs to get the same effect. Physical **addiction** can develop after taking certain **benzodiazepines** for as little as two weeks. Whether they are bought on the street or prescribed by a doctor, the risk is the same. Although doctors now prescribe these drugs less often, many older patients are addicted.

▌Long-term use of sedatives has many risks, including blurred vision and dizziness.

Giving up tranquillizers

People who are addicted to tranquillizers suffer strong **withdrawal symptoms** when they stop taking the drug. These symptoms include anxiety, nausea, headaches, and inability to sleep at night. They may also feel strange sensations and experience **hallucinations**. Up to 15 per cent of people may still have problems even years after giving up the drugs. If someone has been addicted for a long time, they may have to give up the drugs slowly, taking less and less each week until they have given up completely.

Ray's story

Ray was addicted to prescribed tranquillizers for over twenty years. He had many symptoms which his doctor put down to mental illness. Ray changed doctors, and discovered that the symptoms were actually the side effects of the tranquillizers. His new doctor helped him to give up, but Ray suffered strong withdrawal symptoms.

"Just less than two weeks after I stopped taking diazepam [a kind of benzodiazepine] there was an almighty explosion of symptoms. All hell broke loose inside my head and body. The electric shocks that travelled through every nerve ending, particularly in the left side of my body, were extremely frightening. For the first few months I felt as though I was walking uphill through glue on the rolling deck of a ship in a storm with a huge weight pressing down on my head."

35

Anabolic steroids are a group of drugs that all act like the natural male sex hormone **testosterone**. Some people **abuse** them because they think they will improve their looks or performance in sport.

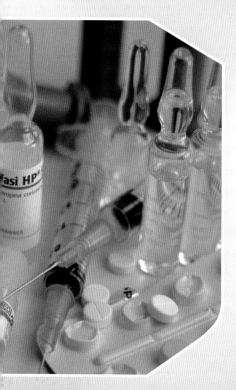

I Doctors usually give anabolic steroids as tablets or by injection.

How do anabolic steroids work?

Anabolic steroids act in the same way as testosterone. Testosterone has two main actions in the body. Firstly, it stops certain tissues from being broken down, including muscle. Secondly, it brings about many of the physical and emotional changes that happen during **puberty**, especially in teenage boys. Anabolic steroid drugs do not act in the same way as the kind of steroids that can be used to treat asthma, arthritis, and eczema (corticosteroids). Both anabolic steroids and corticosteroids are sometimes called just "steroids", which can be confusing.

What are they used for?

There are only a few reasons for doctors to give someone anabolic steroids. A few men and teenage boys cannot make enough of their own testosterone. Anabolic steroids may be used to replace the actions of this sex hormone. Anabolic steroids can also be prescribed for people who are suffering from serious weight loss and muscle wasting, to help them get better. When doctors give anabolic steroids to patients, they watch carefully to make sure the dose is correct.

Steroid abuse

Most of the anabolic steroids that are abused are bought illegally. They are often sold by people who use gyms or who work in the sports industry. People who abuse these drugs are often trying to build up their muscles or improve their sports performance. In the United States, up to 3.5 per cent of 12th grade students, aged 17 or 18, have tried anabolic steroids. Some studies in the United Kingdom suggest that between 5 and 40 per cent of the people in certain gyms have tried these drugs.

"I was at the gym and mentioned to one of the personal trainers that I wished I could put muscle on faster. He said I should try steroids, and offered to get some for me. I made a joke about it, and started talking about something else. But deep down, I was really shocked."

Eddie, aged nineteen

What would you decide to do in a situation like this?

▌At some gyms, a high proportion of the customers may abuse steroids.

Steroids and the heart

Anabolic steroids can be very harmful to the heart and blood vessels. They can raise a person's blood pressure, which means that blood is pumped though the blood vessels with greater force. This can damage the blood vessels and lead to an increased risk of heart attacks and strokes. A stroke can cause death or permanent disability.

Do steroids improve looks?

Steroids can cause many unwanted changes to someone's appearance. They should never be considered a "quick fix" for looks. They can cause hair loss and shrinking testicles in boys, plus growth of breast tissue. They can cause permanent deepening of the voice, shrunken breasts, and facial hair growth in girls. In both sexes, anabolic steroids can make someone have a puffy face and swollen ankles, greasy skin and hair, and severe acne. When people **abuse** anabolic steroids they often take much larger doses than doctors would normally prescribe. This makes it more likely that they will suffer unpleasant **side effects**.

Are there other risks?

Side effects of steroid abuse can include liver and kidney problems. Active people who abuse anabolic steroids may end up training too hard and too often. Top athletes avoid over-training to prevent illness and injury. Many people who abuse anabolic steroids take a mixture of drugs at the same time. Some of these may be legal substances, and some of them may be illegal. Mixing drugs like this makes it more likely that a dangerous reaction will happen inside the body.

Question

Why is steroid abuse so risky for teenagers?

Answer

Anabolic steroids can make the ends of bones harder, which can stunt a teenager's growth.

People who inject steroids sometimes share needles with others. This can cause deadly infections to be passed on from one person to another, including **HIV** (the virus that can cause AIDS) and **hepatitis B** or **C**.

What about mental health?

There are several mental health risks with steroids. They can upset a person's normal sleeping pattern, making them tired and irritable. They can also make a person over-confident and arrogant. Sometimes the drugs can cause strong feelings of depression, **paranoia,** or anxiety that last for months. There is also a strong link between steroids and an increase in aggressive behaviour. This is sometimes called "roid rage".

❚ Anabolic steroids can have a strong effect on someone's mental health, making them feel depressed and anxious.

Ketamine is an **anaesthetic** drug that has been used to make humans and animals unconscious before surgery, and to reduce pain. It is a very powerful drug with strong effects. People who take ketamine without medical advice often experience very unpleasant effects. They can put themselves into a totally helpless state.

Medical uses

Ketamine is now mainly used as an anaesthetic to make animals unconscious before surgery. It is also used as a painkiller for people who have been injured a long way from the nearest hospital, such as on battlefields or in road accidents. It is sometimes called a "dissociative" drug. This means that it makes people feel as if they are far away from their own bodies and separated from what is going on around them.

Ketamine abuse

Most of the ketamine that is sold illegally has been stolen from vets' supplies. It may be sold as a liquid, which is its original medical form. It may also be sold as pills or as a powder. Users sometimes call it "K" or "special K". People sometimes take it at parties, in nightclubs, or at **raves**. There is some evidence to suggest that ketamine **abuse** is on the increase.

Ketamine can cause people to feel as if they're not inside their own body. They may enter a trance-like state or experience **hallucinations**. Hallucinations can be unpleasant or frightening. Ketamine may also cause strong feelings of nausea and people may vomit. Sometimes a person may be awake but unable to move their arms or legs. The most unpleasant experience is sometimes called a "K hole" or "falling into a K hole". This is a terrifying feeling of being completely separated from all the senses.

What are the most serious dangers?

Ketamine is an anaesthetic, so large doses can make a person unconscious. If someone vomits while they are unconscious they can choke to death. There have been a number of reported rapes of victims who were unable to defend themselves because of the effects of ketamine (see also page 33). People who take ketamine are also at risk of injury, for example from stumbling into roads.

Sometimes, people mix ketamine with other drugs such as **opiates** or **sedatives**. This is extremely dangerous as the drugs may act together to stop the heart or lungs from working. Not much is known about the long-term risks of ketamine abuse. However, experts believe it may cause memory loss and mental health problems as well as **psychological dependence**.

❚ Ketamine may make people feel completely disorientated and separated from their surroundings.

Are other prescription drugs abused?

There are a few other **prescription** drugs that people sometimes take without following medical advice. These include **antidepressants** and strong **laxatives**. People sometimes take additional medications to make the effects of other drugs or alcohol stronger. This can cause a fatal reaction.

What are antidepressants?

Antidepressants are drugs that doctors may prescribe to help people who are seriously depressed. These drugs may be part of a treatment plan that also includes **counselling**. The drugs help to bring low levels of certain chemicals in the brain back to normal, which usually helps to improve a patient's mood. Antidepressants usually take two to four weeks to work, as the brain chemicals slowly build back up to normal levels. When a patient has been feeling well again for some time, the drugs are normally reduced over a period of weeks.

These drugs can have **side effects** such as tiredness, dizziness, and anxiety. People who think they are depressed should not try to treat themselves. Only a qualified doctor can decide whether someone needs antidepressants or not.

What are laxatives?

Laxatives are used to treat constipation. They all make the gut empty faster. Side effects include lots of gas in the stomach or guts, and a bloated

Question

Do antidepressants make you feel super happy?

▌Antidepressants should never be taken without the advice of a doctor.

■ Some people are so desperate to lose weight that they turn to drugs, although it is unhealthy and dangerous to do so.

belly. Laxatives are sometimes **abused** by people with eating disorders such as anorexia or bulimia, who think that they can lose weight by getting rid of the food they've eaten. In fact, by the time food has passed into the lower gut, most of the energy (calories or joules) has been absorbed from it already, so it is not going to have much effect on weight. Laxative abuse can damage the gut, making it unable to work properly without more laxatives.

Drugs for sexual problems

Doctors may give Viagra (also called sildenafil) or other similar drugs to some male patients with sexual difficulties. Drugs such as Viagra act to increase blood flow in the tissues of the penis, causing an erection. Side effects include headache, high blood pressure, dizziness, blurred vision, and increased risk of heart attacks. While it might seem cool to try it, or even give it to mates to embarrass them, it is actually very dangerous if it is **misused**.

Answer

No, they just stop you feeling depressed, if a doctor says you're truly depressed in the first place. If you aren't depressed they won't lift your mood at all.

Illegal drug **abuse** does not just affect the life of the person using the drugs. There are wider effects too and many people are forced to pay for the problems of drug abuse and **addiction** in our society.

Who else suffers?

Many people who take drugs say they are not hurting anyone around them, and that the matter is their own private business. However, when someone has a problem with drugs, their whole family suffers. Children may be neglected and relations with family and friends can be strained to breaking point. People suffering from the effects of **prescription** drug abuse often take days off work because of drug-related illnesses.

▌Drug-related emergencies place medical staff under extra pressure.

They can also lose their jobs, which may lead to money problems. Drug users can become drowsy, so they are more likely to have accidents. If someone takes drugs and then drives, they may kill themselves and others.

Medical care

People who have taken accidental **overdoses** need immediate expert medical treatment. Paramedics, doctors, and nurses all have to work hard under pressure to care for them. Drug users often suffer long-term health problems and need many years of expensive care. Many babies born to addicts also need special care and long-term treatment.

What about crime?

Police forces around the world face a big challenge coping with crimes such as **possession** and **supply** of prescription drugs. People who abuse prescription drugs may also commit burglaries. They may break into factories, hospitals, or pharmacies to steal drugs, or into homes to steal money and property. Dealing with these crimes uses up a lot of police time and resources.

Police forces also face the problem of drug-related violence. This may be violence from people who are under the influence of certain drugs. It may be violence between rival drug **dealers** or violence towards people who owe money to dealers.

Police and customs officers have to work hard to prevent **trafficking** and smuggling of prescription drugs. Some of the profits from the sale of illegal drugs help to fund the activities of criminal gangs around the world. Some terrorists are also thought to rely on money from the sale of illegal drugs.

❗ The financial costs

The US National Community Pharmacists Association reports that prescription drug addiction and abuse costs the United States over US$100 billion per year. The Senate Committee on Governmental Affairs says it may be over US$150 billion.

Can drug abuse and addiction be prevented?

Prescription drug **addiction** and **abuse** is a growing problem around the world, and there are many ways that individuals, organizations, and governments are trying to prevent it.

The role of health workers

Health workers have an important role to play in preventing drug abuse and addiction. Doctors and nurses have to work hard to keep up to date with information about medicines, so that they are aware of the risks of certain drugs. They also need to watch their patients carefully for signs of addiction and warn them about the risks. **Pharmacists** have to look out for fake or stolen prescriptions, or patients who might be addicted to their medication. Health services and charitable organizations can educate the public about the risks of drug abuse, and provide treatment and support to help people give up drugs.

❙ Many schools and youth groups run drug education programmes to help prevent drug abuse. Here students are discussing how to handle **peer pressure**.

What else can be done?

Governments around the world work hard to prevent and tackle the problem of prescription drug abuse and addiction. Recently, many countries have introduced strict border controls to prevent drug smuggling and **trafficking**. Many police forces have drug squads, with officers who are specially trained to track down illegal drug **dealers**.

Some schools and youth groups have special visits from organizations that educate young people about drug use. Many schools provide lessons about drugs where students are encouraged to discuss the issue. It is also important for individual people to educate themselves about healthy lifestyles. They need to be aware of the true risks of illegal drugs.

Needle exchange programmes

In many countries, needle exchange programmes have been set up to help reduce the risks associated with the sharing of needles. These programmes involve collecting and destroying used needles and providing users with new clean needles. There is evidence that these programmes can significantly reduce the number of people who become infected by the **HIV** virus through sharing needles.

Viewpoints

Some people believe that needle exchange programmes are an important way of preventing harm caused by drug abuse. Other people are not in favour of them.

- **Needle exchange programmes make life healthier for everyone**
  Needle exchanges have been successful in reducing the spread of diseases such as HIV. This protects the people who take the drugs, but it also protects the general public as well. While drug users are at the exchange, they can be given information about how to give up drugs.

- **Needle exchange programmes allow drug users to keep taking drugs**
  These programmes send out a message that there is a safe way to take drugs. They make it easier for people to continue being drug addicts. Taking illegal drugs is a crime, not an illness.

What do you think?

Giving up prescription drugs

People who have drug problems may need a wide range of advice, help, and support, but may not always know how to find this help. Fortunately, there are many organizations that offer help and several kinds of treatment.

Giving up drugs

Many drug users want information about drug safety, advice about the law, and a safe place to talk about what they're going through. If someone is **addicted** to **prescription** drugs and wants to give them up, it's a good idea for them to talk to a doctor or nurse who knows all about addiction. If they have been taking the prescription drugs for a long time, it could be dangerous to stop taking them suddenly. They will need advice about how to reduce the daily amount slowly.

Staying off drugs

Once someone has given up drugs, they may need support to help them stay off the drugs. Many people find **counselling** very helpful. During counselling people can talk about their problems and seek out new ways to cope that do not involve drugs.

Marissa's story

Marissa was addicted to prescription painkillers, but later gave them up and joined a support group called Narcotics Anonymous. Other ex-users gave her support and helped her to stay off drugs.

*"If I start to feel overwhelmed I seek out the support of someone, instead of isolating myself and thinking about using drugs. When I feel bad sometimes I go to a Narcotics Anonymous meeting. I am staying **clean** by working to get that person back who was happy without drugs. I feel motivated to keep my life on the right track and utilize the potential I have."*

After a period of addiction, people also need help putting their lives back together. This includes improving family relationships, mending friendships, and getting back into education or work. They might need to find new ways to express themselves or enjoy their free time. This whole process is called **rehabilitation**.

❚ Many ex-addicts find that group meetings help them to stay away from drugs.

Who can help?

The family doctor or nurse is often a good place to start, because they can contact other organizations for patients. Many hospitals and clinics have specialist units where people can be treated for drug **dependence**, staying overnight if they need to. There are also many drug agencies that offer advice, or have useful websites or confidential phone lines. People are often able to turn to family and friends for support too.

Are there things that worry you about **prescription** drugs? Maybe you are worried about somebody else who might be using drugs? There are many people and organizations that can give you the right information.

Information close to home

If you have any concerns or questions about drugs, there may be a nurse or **counsellor** at your school you could talk to.

▐ Prescription drug abuse is not part of a healthy lifestyle.

You can make an appointment to have a chat with them **in confidence**, and you won't get into trouble for asking questions. Your town or school library may stock books about drugs too. There's a list of suggested further reading on page 55 of this book.

Finding out more

There are many organizations that provide information about drugs. Some of these organizations are listed on pages 54–55 of this book. You can contact them for help or information even in the middle of the night. It might seem hard to talk, but it's a good thing to do. You'll feel much better talking about your concerns. And people who have been trained to give support and advice are very understanding and helpful.

Worried about someone else?

If you're worried about someone else's drug use, there are many organizations you can contact for help and support. You can ring one of their helplines and talk to a trained counsellor. You don't have to bottle your feelings up and cope on your own.

It's up to you

Are you worried that someone might one day offer you drugs such as **amphetamines**, **opiates**, or **anabolic steroids**? You need to think very hard about what your decision would mean to you. Taking these drugs for non-medical reasons can really ruin your life.

! Coping with pressure

Many young people are offered drugs. If you have a plan for coping with this situation, it is much easier to say "no". If you're offered drugs you can:

- say "no" or "no thanks" as many times as you need to

- change the subject to stop the other person talking about drugs

- say that taking drugs is a bad idea.

If they keep bothering you, you can:

- tell them that a real friend would respect your decision

- walk away from the person, or move to stand with people who you feel comfortable with.

If they still keep bothering you, you can:

- spend less time with that person

- avoid the place or situation where it happened.

Glossary

abuse use of drugs for non-medical reasons in a way that has a bad effect on the person's health or body

addiction when a person is dependent on (unable to manage without) a drug and finds it extremely hard to stop using it

amphetamine type of stimulant drug that speeds up the activity of the brain

anabolic steroid type of strong synthetic hormone drug. Anabolic steroids are sometimes taken by sportspeople because they believe they will make their muscles stronger.

anaesthetic drug that removes the sensation of pain

antidepressant drug used to treat depression

benzodiazepine type of sedative drug (also called a minor tranquillizer), which causes someone to become calm or sleepy

clean not taking drugs

coma state of deep unconsciousness from which it is very hard or even impossible to wake a person

counselling advice and guidance given to people to help resolve their problems

craving strong or uncontrollable need or longing

dealer person who buys and sells drugs illegally

dependence when a person is unable to cope without a drug

depressant substance that slows down the activity of the brain and the body

fix dose of a drug to which one is addicted

hallucination experience of seeing or hearing something that is not really present and only exists in the mind

hepatitis B and C diseases caused by a virus that can seriously damage the liver

HIV virus that can lead to AIDS

hooked addicted

illegal manufacture making drugs illegally without a government licence

in confidence privately, without telling anyone else

ketamine synthetic anaesthetic drug which can cause hallucinations

laxative drug that makes the bowels empty faster

minor tranquillizer type of sedative drug

misuse use of something for the wrong purpose or in the wrong way

narcotic type of drug that relieves pain; also refers to an illegal addictive drug

nervous system the brain, spinal column, and network of nerves, which together control a person's thoughts, feelings, and movements

opiate type of drug that relieves pain, also called a narcotic

overdose excessive dose of a drug which the body cannot cope with

panic attack sudden very strong feeling of anxiety, which makes a person's heart race

paranoia mental condition involving feelings of suspicion and distrust – a sense that everyone is out to get you, or to criticize your behaviour or actions

peer influence or **pressure** influence or pressure to do something to fit in with a group of friends

pharmacist trained person who prepares and dispenses drugs

possession owning or having an illegal drug (either carrying it or having it hidden somewhere)

prescription instruction written by a doctor or dentist which authorizes a pharmacist to issue a drug to a patient

psychological dependence when a person feels they need drugs to get through everyday life and cannot cope without them

puberty period during which adolescents develop sexual maturity

rave large party or gathering involving dancing, especially to electronic dance music

recreational use use of drugs on an occasional basis, especially when socializing

rehabilitation process of returning to ordinary healthy life after a period of addiction

sedative drug that causes someone to become calm or sleepy

side effect unwanted effect of a drug or medical treatment

snort take a drug by sniffing it up the nose

spiking practice of adding alcohol or other drugs to a person's drink without the knowledge of the person who will be drinking it

stimulant drug that speeds up the activity of the brain, making people feel alert and full of energy

supply give or sell drugs to other people

synthetic made artificially using chemicals

testosterone the main male sex hormone

tolerance needing larger and larger doses of a drug to get the same effect

toxic poisonous

trafficking smuggling or transporting drugs, usually in large amounts and across the borders of different countries

tranquillizer type of sedative drug, which causes someone to become calm or sleepy

withdrawal symptoms unpleasant physical and mental feelings experienced during the process of giving up an addictive drug

There are a number of organizations that provide information and advice about drugs. Some have helpful websites, or provide information packs and leaflets. Others offer help and support over the phone.

Contacts in the UK

Adfam
Waterbridge House, 32–36 Loman Street, London SE1 0EH
Tel: 020 7928 8898
www.adfam.org.uk
Adfam is a national charity that gives confidential support and information to families and friends of drug users. They also run family support groups.

CITA (Council for Involuntary Tranquillizer Addiction)
The JDI Centre, 3–11 Mersey View, Waterloo, Liverpool L22 6QA
Helpline: 0151 932 0102 (10 a.m.–1 p.m. Mon–Fri)
CITA helps patients and their families to cope with addiction to benzodiazapines and withdrawal from these drugs. The helpline is staffed by nurses and counsellors.

Connexions Direct
Helpline: 080 800 13219 (8 a.m.–2 a.m. daily)
Text: 07766 4 13219
www.connexions-direct.com
This service for young people aged thirteen to nineteen offers information and advice on a wide range of topics, including drugs.

DrugScope
32–36 Loman Street, London SE1 0EE
Tel: 020 7928 1211
www.drugscope.org.uk
A national drugs information agency with services that include a library, a wide range of publications, and a website.

Families Anonymous
Doddington & Rollo Community Association, Charlotte Despard Avenue, Battersea, London SW11 5HD
Helpline: 0845 1200 660
www.famanon.org.uk
An organization involved in support groups for parents and families of drug users. They can put you in touch with groups in different parts of the country.

FRANK
Tel: 0800 776600
Email: frank@talktofrank.com
www.talktofrank.com
An organization for young people that gives free, confidential advice and information about drugs 24 hours a day.

Narcotics Anonymous
UK Service Office, 202 City Road, London EC1V 2PH
Helpline: 020 7730 0009 (10 a.m.–10 p.m. daily)
www.ukna.org
A fellowship of people who have given up narcotics, using a twelve-step programme similar to the one used by Alcoholics Anonymous.

Release
Helpline: 0845 4500 215 (10 a.m.–5.30 p.m. Mon–Fri)
Email: ask@release.org.uk
www.release.org.uk
An organization that provides legal advice to drug users, their families, and friends. The advice is free, professional, non-judgmental, and confidential.

Contacts in Australia and New Zealand

Alcohol & Other Drugs Council of Australia (ADCA)
17 Napier Close, Deakin, ACT 2600
Tel: 02 6281 1002
www.adca.org.au
ADCA works to prevent or reduce the harm caused by drugs.

Australian Drug Foundation
409 King Street, West Melbourne, VIC 3003
Tel: 03 9278 8100
www.adf.org.au
An organization that works to prevent and reduce drug problems.

The DARE (Drug Abuse Resistance Education) Foundation of New Zealand
PO Box 50744, Porirua, New Zealand
Tel: 04 238 9550
www.dare.org.nz
An organization that provides drug prevention education programmes.

Foundation for Alcohol and Drug Education (FADE)
9 Anzac Street, PO Box 33–1505, Takapuna, Auckland, New Zealand
Tel: 09 489 1719
www.fade.org.nz
A national organization that provides services and information throughout the country.

Narcotics Anonymous
Australian Service Office, 1st Floor, 204 King Street, Newtown, NSW 2042
National helpline: 1300 652 820
http://na.org.au/
The Australian division of Narcotics Anonymous has helplines for users and their friends and relatives, plus events and meetings around Australia.

Turning Point
54–62 Gertrude Street, Fitzroy, VIC 3065
Helpline (DirectLine): 1800 888 236
www.turningpoint.org.au
Turning Point provides specialist treatment and support services to people affected by alcohol and drugs.

Further reading

Dr Miriam Stoppard's Drug Information File: From Alcohol and Tobacco to Ecstasy and Heroin, by Miriam Stoppard (Dorling Kindersley, 1999)

Drugs and You, by Bridget Lawless (Heinemann Library, 2000)

Drugs: The Truth, by Aidan Macfarlane and Ann McPherson (Oxford University Press, 2003)

Health Issues: Drugs, by Sarah Lennard-Brown (Hodder Children's Books, 2004)

Just the Facts: Drugs in Sport, by Clive Gifford (Heinemann Library, 2003)

Need to Know: Painkillers and Tranquillizers, by Michael Durham (Heinemann Library, 2003)

Teen Issues: Drugs, by Joanna Watson and Joanna Kedge (Raintree, 2004)

Why Do People Take Drugs?, by Patsy Westcott (Hodder Children's Books, 2000)

Wise Guides: Drugs, by Anita Naik (Hodder Children's Books, 1997)

Further research

If you want to find out more about the problems related to prescription drug abuse, you can search the Internet, using a search engine such as Google. Try using keywords such as:

Prescription + drugs
Opiates + law
Stimulants + dependence
Steroids + sport

Index

accidents 32, 45
addiction 4, 6, 7, 8, 12–13,
    15, 16, 44, 46, 47
    amphetamines 29
    opiates 18, 22, 23
    sedatives (tranquillizers)
    30, 31, 34
    stimulants 24
    treatment for 15, 48–49
ADHD 24, 25
advice 48–49, 50–51
aggression 26, 34, 39
alcohol 6, 7, 8, 12, 32, 33
amphetamines 16, 24–29,
    51
anabolic steroids 7, 11, 16,
    36–39, 51
anaesthetics 40–41
antidepressants 42, 43
anxiety 11, 22, 23, 26, 29,
    30, 34, 39, 42

babies 21, 27, 45
benzodiazepines 16, 31, 32,
    34
brain 20, 24, 26, 30, 32, 42

codeine 18
constipation 18, 26, 34, 42
corticosteroids 36
counselling 42, 48, 50–51
cravings 22
crime 14–17, 22, 23, 45
crystal meth 25

dealers 4, 9, 15, 19, 29, 45,
    47; see also supplying
deaths 16, 19, 20, 27, 32, 33,
    38, 41, 42
Deca-Durabolin 36
dependence see addiction;
    psychological dependence
depressants 30–35
depression 11, 22, 26, 28,
    29, 39, 43
diarrhoea 22, 26, 34
driving 20, 32, 45

eating disorders 43
education 20, 46, 47
emergencies 21, 44, 45
ephedra 26, 27

Gamma Hydroxybutyrate
    (GHB) 33
giving up 4, 22, 23, 29, 34,
    48–49

hallucinations 26, 34, 40
headaches 18, 34, 43
heart 24, 27, 32, 38, 41, 43
help 48–49, 50–51
hepatitis 21, 39
heroin 8, 9, 18, 19
HIV 21, 39, 47

injecting 19, 21, 25, 32, 39,
    47

ketamine 40–41

law 14–17, 45
laxatives 42–43

memory 31, 34, 41
mental health 26, 39, 41
minor tranquillizers see
    tranquillizers
mixing drugs 6, 7, 11, 21, 27,
    32, 38, 41
morphine 18, 19
muscles 23, 30, 36

narcolepsy 24–25
narcotics see opiates
nausea 20, 23, 34, 40
needles 21, 39
    needle exchange 47

opiates 4, 7, 9, 16, 18–23, 41,
    51
overdose 7, 18, 20, 24, 31,
    32, 45
OxyContin 19

painkillers 9, 12, 40, 48;
    see also opiates
panic 23, 26
paranoia 26, 39
peer influence or pressure
    10–11, 46, 51
pharmacists 5, 9, 12, 46
physical addiction 12, 22,
    29, 34
possession 14, 15, 16, 45
pregnancy 20, 21, 27

psychological dependence
    12, 22, 29, 41; see also
    addiction

rape 33, 41
raves 40
rehabilitation 49
relationships 13, 20, 22, 44,
    49
Ritalin 25, 28
Rohypnol 33
"roid rage" 39

sedatives 7, 9, 11, 12, 16,
    30–35, 41
side effects 6, 7, 11, 20–21,
    24, 28, 31, 34–35, 38, 42,
    43
sleep problems 23, 26, 30,
    39, 34
smuggling 17, 45, 47
"speed" see amphetamines
spiking 33
sports 7, 11, 17, 37
stealing 13, 19, 22, 23, 45
steroids see anabolic
    steroids
stimulants 7, 9, 11, 16,
    24–29
stomach 23, 26, 34, 42–43
street drugs 8, 9, 17, 24, 28,
    29
supplying 4, 9, 14–15, 16,
    19, 21, 37, 45; see also
    dealers

telephone helplines 51
terrorism 45
testosterone 36
tolerance 22, 29, 34
trafficking 15, 45, 47
tranquillizers 30–35

"uppers" see amphetamines

Valium 30
Viagra 43
vomiting 20, 23, 34, 40, 41

weight loss 36, 43
Winstrol 36
withdrawal symptoms 12,
    22, 23, 34, 35